Simple steps into spraying

Book 1 - airless

Pete Wilkinson

First published in the United Kingdom in 2021

Copyright © Peter Wilkinson

Peter Wilkinson has asserted his right to be identified as the author of this work in accordance with the Copyright, Designs and Patents Act 1988

All rights reserved. No part of this publication may be reproduced, stored in a retrieval system, or transmitted in any form or by any means, electronic, mechanical, photocopying, recording or otherwise, without prior permission of the copyright owner.

2021 Edition

09-03-2021

First edition

Dedicated to all those decorators getting into spraying

Contents

Step 1 – Deciding to spray

Step 2 – Why use airless?

Step 3 – Which airless sprayer?

Step 4 – Setting the sprayer up

Step 5 – What is a good surface to learn on?

Step 6 – Actually spraying

Step 7 – Cleaning out the sprayer

Step 8 – Thinking about accessories

Finally – summing up

Step 1

Deciding to spray

If you are reading this book, then I assume that you are a decorator and that you have never sprayed. It is something that you have heard a lot about but have not done yourself. You want to investigate spraying but you don't want to spend a fortune in money and time before you take it any further.

If you decide that you want to explore spraying a little further, then you need to know which sprayer to buy and have a simple guide on how to use it. You have been on YouTube and Facebook but it's all a bit confusing and there is a lot of conflicting information.

Before you carry on you may be wondering who I am and why you should bother listening to me. I have been a decorator all my life and I have also taught painting and decorating at a local college to apprentices. I now run a private training company called "PaintTech Training Academy" and we specialise in training decorators to be sprayers.

Our motto is "decorators teaching decorators" because we still carry out contracts and we know what kinds of problems that you will come across when spraying because we too have had to deal with them.

I have a number of books on decorating and spraying on Amazon (search "Fast and Flawless") if you need more information after reading this then check them out.

Right, back to the main plot.

You have heard about spraying, but you are undecided if it's for you. You have heard good things about it (you can make more money) but you have also heard horror stories (overspray).

I am not going to spend too long here on the horror stories, I cover all this in other books but what I do want to look at are the reasons that you should think about getting into spraying.

There are a few reasons, but I will focus on three.

First, it's faster

Roughly translated this means that you will make more money. How much faster depends on the type of job that you are doing. If you are spraying out a warehouse and it is 10,000 m^2 then it will be 10 times faster.

If you are spraying a lounge ceiling, then it might only be twice as fast as using a brush and roller.

I speak to a lot of decorators, so I know what the common objections to this are, things like "Is it worth setting a sprayer up just to paint a lounge ceiling?" or "does it not just use loads more paint when painting a warehouse?" or "what about the overspray!" but in the end, all of these are not issues once you get confident with a sprayer.

When I was much younger, I was lucky enough to win a trip over to the States, while I was out there, I spoke to several painting contractors and I found that the painters earn much more over there than we do over here.

It took me a number of years to really fathom this out, but I now realise that a lot of the work over there is sprayed and therefore they turn out much more work per day than we do, and this means that they earn more money.

How much more money?

Well, it depends of course on how experienced they are, what type of work they do and what kind of prices that they charge.

But because I know that this is the question that you really want to answer then I will say that you could double what you currently earn. So, if you earn £600 a week then you could earn £1200 a week.

I know a few decorators than have made the move from brushing and rolling over to spraying and that is the typical increase in earnings.

What I will say is that it is a learning curve. You cannot buy a sprayer on Monday and be earning a grand a week on Tuesday. That is not how the world works.

You will have to get your head around it and get comfortable with it. This may take a year, or it may take a month, it depends on what you are like at picking new skills up.

I think that the main decision is "do I want to go down the spraying road or not?" You can start down the road and it may take you ten years to get fully up to speed, it does not matter. You can still brush and roll stuff after you have bought a sprayer.

Bear in mind though that I think this is the way the industry is going in this country and in ten years' time if everyone is spraying and you are not then you will find it very difficult to compete and you may find your earnings drop.

I think that over time the industry is going to split into two (much like most other countries) and there will be high earning sprayers and very low earning brush painters.

Secondly the finish is amazing.

This is the real reason that I love spraying, the finish. Customers love it too. When you spray the woodwork in someone's house the finish is perfect, the customer has never seen anything like it before and they will not stop talking about it.

That means that you will find that you will get more work from your existing customers. It also means that it is easier to compete against other decorators because it is less likely that they will offer the same level of finish as you.

Finally, it's fun

Yes, I know, work is not meant to be fun, you are there to make money. I have trained many decorators on site to spray and the one thing I notice is that I cannot get the gun back off them and they are loving to spray. They have a big grin on their face.

This is the hidden benefit of spraying. I have been spraying commercially now for many years and I still get that fun factor.

Hopefully you are still with me and you are thinking "mmm yeah I can see myself doing this", if that is the case then let's go to step 2.

Step 2

Why use airless?

If you have started to look into spraying, then you will know that it's a bit of a minefield. There are all sorts of sprayers out there. People will give you all sorts of advice too, usually based on what they are doing.

I am one of those people, I like airless sprayers and it is what I use 99% of the time when I am decorating. Let me explain why I like it so much and what kind of work that I do and then you can decide if it is for you.

An airless sprayer is simply a paint pump. It pumps the paint (at very high pressure) to the spray gun. In the gun is a spray tip. The tip is a little tiny hole that causes the paint to turn into a mist. No air is used to atomise the paint.

All other spray systems use air to atomise the paint, airless doesn't, hence the name.

The main advantage of an airless system is speed.

You can buy various sizes of airless sprayer (more on this in step 3) and they are rated by how fast they deliver the paint. For example, 2.5 litres a minute. This means that if I pull the trigger on the gun after 1 minute, I have applied 2.5 litres of paint.

Amazing eh?

I will talk more about this when we look at which is the best sprayer for you to buy.

When I spray out student apartments it usually takes me around 5 minutes to spray the ceiling and walls in the apartments. This is pretty fast, and no other spraying system could achieve this speed. It means that if you have a few to do then you will get through the work in double quick time.

Another advantage is that the sprayer has a suction tube that draws the paint out of a big bucket. Typically, a 20-litre bucket. This means that you do not have to fill up the paint every couple of minutes.

In fairness if you are in the zone and spraying out an apartment every 5 or 6 minutes then you will have to fill the bucket up every 15 minutes however if you have a little paint pot attached to the gun then it would only last 2 minutes. This is a big advantage of airless.

Another advantage is the gun. The gun is light and easy to hold. You can get in into some quite tight areas with ease. Because the paint container is not attached to the gun it is easy to work with.

Finally, the biggest advantage to me is that you can spray any surface with any paint without thinning the paint. I will discuss paint thinning in later steps and where I do and don't thin paint.

For now, all you need to know that it will spray more or less any paint straight out of the tin. This is a big advantage if you are just working with standard decorative paints like Crown and Dulux.

Any surface means just that, any surface. I can take my little airless sprayer onto a job and spray the ceiling and the walls with emulsion. Then clean out the sprayer and put it into acrylic satin and spray the skirtings, the doors, the staircase and the window cills. Amazing, all with one sprayer and at lightning speed.

All this sounds a bit too good to be true and in fairness there is a slight drawback. Airless is quite a skill if you are going to do more than just mist coat. Learning to spray with an airless sprayer is a bit like learning to drive in a Ferrari. It's fast and it's hard to control when you are learning. However, once you get past the OMG stage and get it under control you just would not want to go back to driving a Ford Focus.

I would advise doing a course to get you on the right track, mind you I would say that because I teach spraying, if you are interested then email us at courses@painttechtrainingacademy.co.uk

I have included our course leaflets at the back of the book so you can have a look and see what you fancy.

If you decide not to do a course and just get to grips with it yourself then of course you can do. Just expect the process to take some time and don't try and run before you can walk.

Some people take to it like a duck to water and others take more time to get their head around it. By the way I am one of those people that it took some time for, I am by no means "a natural".

One final word of caution is that airless can be dangerous and needs to be treated with respect. If you are careless then you can accidentally inject yourself with paint because of the very high 2000psi pressure.

The problem with this is that paint is toxic and very difficult to get out of your hand or arm once that it is in there.

It is an immediate surgery job because the paint will start to make it's way through your system and while the surgeon can amputate your hand, they cannot amputate your heart or brain.

Have a look on your YouTube and see what I mean. If this puts you off then maybe go down another road, check out HVLP as this is completely safe.

Bear in mind that driving your van is pretty dangerous these days too, especially on the M6, but you drive with care so that you stay safe and you can spray with care too, just make sure you know what you are doing, an airless sprayer is not a toy.

If I have convinced you that airless is the way to go for you then we need to look at what sprayer we should buy to start us off on our spraying journey. Let us move onto to step 3.

Step 3

Which airless sprayer?

When I teach decorators on our airless spraying course the most common question I am asked is "which sprayer shall I buy."

My usual reply to this is to ask what the decorator's budget is. Before we look at this let me ask you a question.

If you were buying a new van what would your budget be? £300?

No that would be ridiculous wouldn't it. You would probably be looking at spending £2,000 minimum and if you were feeling really flush maybe even a new van. Now I know what you are thinking, "I cannot run my business without a van, it's essential, it makes me money."

Well, I can tell you that I cannot run my business without a sprayer and also it makes me more money that a van would.

So why are we only prepared to spend £300?

Because we are not completely convinced it is worth it, that's why.

Decorators really deliberate over what their first sprayer will be, and I get this because I was the same. Let me tell you a little secret, every decorator I know that is a sprayer has more than one. In most cases they have 5 or 6.

Why?

Well two reasons. First, you are making more money and you need to spend it on something right, buying new kit is great and buying new sprayers is no different. Secondly you realise that the sprayer is an investment and will actually pay for itself many times over.

Okay so I will answer the question properly now.

First, decide your budget. If its £300 then I suggest you save up a bit more. The three budget bands I will look at are £1000, £1500 and £2,000.

There are two types of airless sprayer out there, ones made for the DIY market and ones that are designed for the professional. The DIY ones are fine, but they are only designed for DIY and that means very little use. How can you tell if it is a DIY sprayer? Dead easy, it will be cheap. Less than £500.

Next, we need to talk about brands of sprayer. There are a number of brands out there. In my opinion all the brands that make professional sprayers are good. So, find the brand that you like and maybe stick with them.

To keep it really simple I am going to choose one brand and that is Graco. Why have I chosen Graco? They are the market leader, and they have sprayers in every category. To balance things off a bit at the end I will show you my own sprayer and explain why I bought it.

Entry level budget £1000

Above – The Graco GXFF

This is the Graco GXFF and is very popular with decorators starting out into spraying. This will cost around £800 - £1000 with accessories.

The advantages are that it is light and easy to carry. The hopper is really handy especially if you are spraying small amounts of paint.

The disadvantage is that is only delivers 1.5 litres a minute and therefore it is a little underpowered. It will spray most paints, but you will need to thin them to get them to atomise properly, especially undercoats, satins and glosses.

Mid-range budget - £1500

Personally, I would go for a sprayer that is a little more powerful and the Graco 390 hits the spot. It has a flow rate of 1.8 litres per minute and is still a handy sprayer.

You can use it with the suction hose which means sprayer larger quantities is easier, but you can also add a hopper and this makes it a great woodwork sprayer.

The great thing about this sprayer is that when you go and buy your second bigger sprayer then this still makes a great second machine that you will use alongside your bigger sprayer.

Above – The Graco 390

Bigger budget - £2000

Above – The Graco 495 ST Max

The Graco 495 ST Max. This sprayer will do everything that you would need as a decorator. It has a delivery rate of 2.3 litres a minute which is plenty, and it will work all day long spraying thousands of litres.

This sprayer also has a "pro exchange" pump which means when the time comes for a service then you can just take out the old pump and replace it with a new one yourself easily and cheaply. This basically makes your sprayer brand new again.

I hope this gives you a simple guide to what is out there. All brands make sprayers in the three price bands. If you look at the flow rate, then that will help you compare.

Many sprayers will have a recommended tip size that they will go up to. Be careful with this because many are optimistic. I will talk about tip sizes later.

What sprayer do I have?

Well even though it was a stretch I decided to break the bank and spend over £2,000 on a sprayer and I bought the Tritech T7.

This sprayer is built like a tank, it has a flow rate of 2.9 litres a minute which is plenty, and it has never missed a beat. I have had this sprayer for 5 years and I still do not regret spending the money.

I have used it on very large jobs, and it has sprayed 100's of apartments. Tritech do not make an entry level machine so even though I recommend it to people many do not have the big budget needed to buy one.

These decorators will look at manufacturers who make a wider range of airless sprayers such as Graco.

Above – The Tritech T7

Just to sum up, I am not going to say spend as much as you can.

If you can comfortably afford £2,000 then I would spend that, if you can't then buy a smaller machine and work your way up. A smaller machine will always get used and it will make you the money that you need to get a bigger one.

Just as a side note I have a little Qtech QT190 (see picture on the next page) and it is my most used sprayer even though it is small it is very handy, and I use it a lot. These are only £600. Obviously if I had to choose just one sprayer to keep then it would be the T7.

I have every brand of airless sprayer and they all have something that I like about them and something that bugs me, so my advice is to shop around and find a sprayer that suits you.

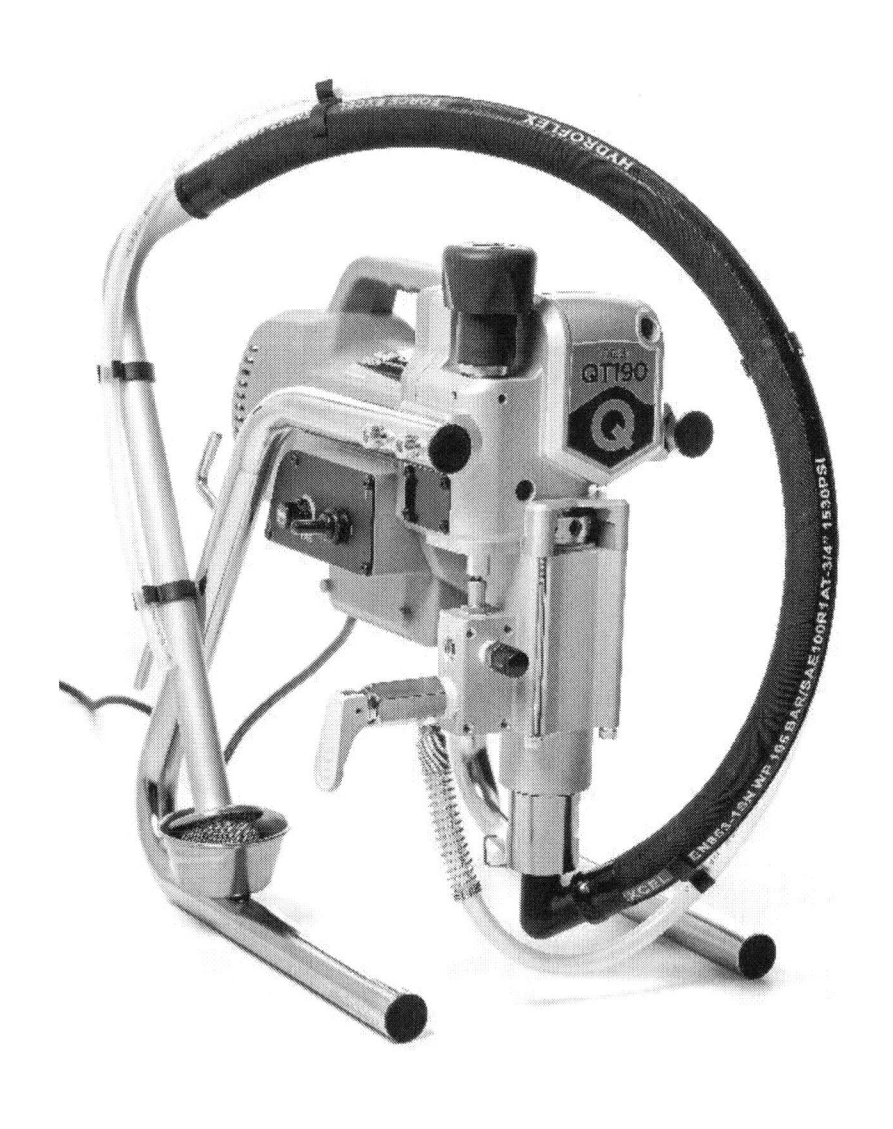

Above – The handy little QT190

Step 4

Setting the sprayer up

"Is it really worth spraying that ceiling? By the time you have set up the sprayer I could have rolled it."

If I had a pound each time that a decorator said this to me, I would have retired years ago. What they really mean is by the time *they* have set the sprayer up because I can set my sprayer up in around a minute.

It just takes some practice to get there, it's surprising though, set you your sprayer every day for a month and you have pretty much nailed it.

What I suggest is that you write the steps on a bit of masking tape and stick it to the top of your sprayer as a crutch to help you as you learn.

I am going to try and make this easy.

First, I will give you the steps to setting up the sprayer and then I will give you a little more detail. I am assuming that you have taken the sprayer out of the box and connected the gun and hose.

I also assume that if it is brand new that you have flushed out the oil that the sprayer is stored in with warm soapy water.

I have a habit of trying the sprayer in water too if I have not used it for a while just to be sure that it is working fine before I put it into paint. I am going to assume that you have a hopper on the sprayer too although it makes no difference to the steps when setting up.

A final word on tips and filters. You will most likely have a 50-mesh filter and a 517 tip so we will play with these to start with. If you want to find out more about the nitty gritty of airless spraying, then I suggest checking out my first book "Fast and Flawless – a guide to airless spraying".

The next page outline the steps to setting up the sprayer.

STAGE 1 – Prime the sprayer

Step 1 – Plug the sprayer in (obviously)

Step 2 – Pour the paint into the hopper.

Step 3 – Turn the "prime/spray" switch to "PRIME" and turn on the sprayer, turn the pressure up.

Step 4 – Once primed (it takes about 10 seconds) turn down the pressure to zero and switch off for a second to think.

I am going to stop for a second.

This next bit is not complicated but it may seem like it is.

You will have water in the hose from when you cleaned it out. You need to clear the water from the hose and fill it with paint.

To do this you will have to turn the sprayer to "SPRAY" but when you do this the pressure will build up. You do not want that at this stage because you want to run the water into a bucket and if it's under pressure that will be very messy.

Take the tip and tip guard off the gun, this will make this stage easier.

You need to pull the trigger on the gun BEFORE you turn to "SPRAY" so that the pressure cannot build up.

Then slowly turn the pressure up and the water will start to run out of the hose. I have outlined this on the next page.

STAGE 2 – Flush out the water until you get paint

Step 5 – Turn the sprayer back on.

Step 6 – Point the gun into an empty bucket and pull the trigger.

Step 7 – Switch the "Primer/spray" switch to "SPRAY" and turn the pressure up slowly.

Step 8 – The water will run out of the gun as the paint makes its way along the hose. This will take about 30 seconds.

Step 9 – Once you see paint, turn the pressure down and switch off.

STAGE 3 – Test the spray pattern

Step 10 – Switch on the sprayer, switch to "SPRAY", and turn the pressure up.

This time the pressure will build up, the gauge will show this and once up to pressure the sprayer will go quiet.

Step 11 – Spray a test area of wall to see what the spray pattern is like. You want it nice and solid.

Step 12 – Turn up the pressure until the spray pattern is like a letter box. (See picture next page).

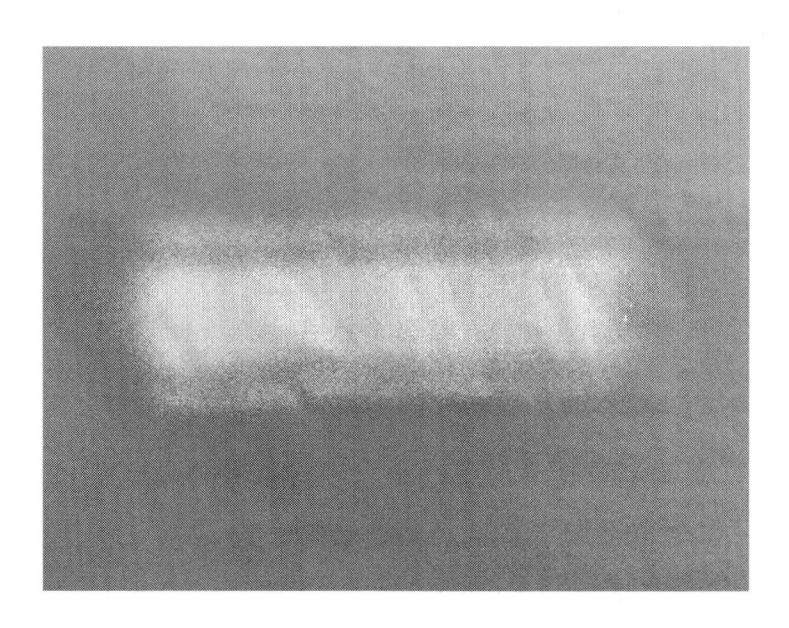

Above – tails, not enough pressure

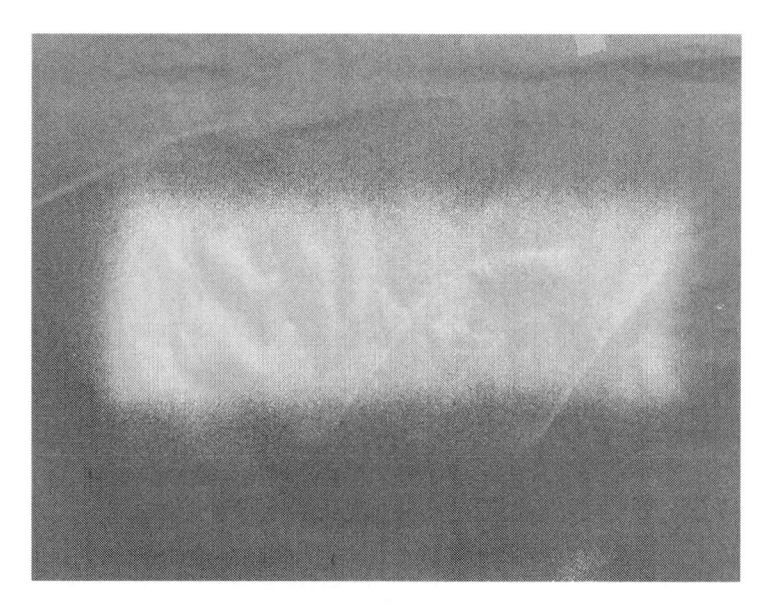

Above - A nice spray pattern

The last stage is important. If the paint is not atomising enough then you can do two things.

1. Turn the pressure up until the pattern is solid.

2. If you are at full pressure and you still have tails, then you can thin the paint.

Another top tip is that warm paint is better than freezing cold so if you can get the paint up to room temperature then this helps a lot. You can get heated hoses but that's more advanced and more expense.

To summarise.

1. Prime the sprayer
2. Flush the water out of the hose
3. Test the spray pattern until correct.

Easy.

Don't over think it. If it is your first time setting up, take your sprayer outside and practice with water first to get a feel for how the spray/prime swich works and how the sprayer feels when it is spraying. This will help take away the fear as well. Maybe spend all afternoon doing this.

When you are under pressure to paint a job, this is not the time to start learning. Do it one Sunday afternoon when it does not matter if you struggle a little.

I have a YouTube video setting up a Graco GXFF so maybe search "Pete Wilkinson Decorators" and check this out.

Once you get to this stage you have got further than many decorators and from now on it gets more fun and easier.

I think the fear factor is what holds us all back from getting into spraying and once you get to this stage you will wonder what you were bothered about.

Step 5

What is a good surface to learn on?

Okay; this is not really a step is it? I wanted to discuss this before we carry on because I think it is important. I know many decorators who buy a sprayer, have a go with it for one day, have a disaster of a day and then give up.

The sprayer is thrown in the shed never to be seen again except in conversation, "Oh yes I have an airless sprayer somewhere in my shed, I have only used it once."

Why does this happen?

Well, I think one of the reasons is that we can be a little too ambitious when we start off. Some surfaces are harder to spray than others and some are easy. Also, if you are spraying a combination of surfaces such as ceilings, walls, and woodwork it can complicate things even more.

The easiest surface to spray is a bare one, because this is very absorbent and if you put a little too much paint on (beginners usually do) then it will not run.

Ceilings are also very easy because they are flat and have very little masking, they will generally not run if you put too much paint on.

I always recommend two surfaces to start off on, these are bare plaster (mist coating) and ceilings. The ceilings do not have to be bare plaster and I would start spraying every ceiling from now on.

It's great practice setting the sprayer up and cleaning it out, there is very little masking, and the finish is amazing on a ceiling.

Many decorators ask me how I would protect the carpet if I was spraying a ceiling in a carpeted room. My answer is always "How would YOU protect the carpet if you were rolling the ceiling?"

"I would put a dust sheet down" they reply.

"I would put a dust sheet down" I reply too.

A roller is much messier than a sprayer. With a roller you get blobs and splatters of paint. With a sprayer you get dust. By the time the atomised emulsion reaches the floor it has dried to a dust.

At first you will not feel like getting the sprayer out to paint just a ceiling and you will resist. But if you do this every time for a couple of months, I guarantee you that you will never want to go back to rolling a ceiling. You just have to power through.

The other surface mentioned above is bare plaster. Ideally a full house with bare plaster walls and ceilings. You can thin the emulsion down and mist coat the lot.

If you are lucky the electrician has not fitted the sockets and lights and you will have very little masking to do. Its great practice, you cannot go far wrong and its great fun. Fast too of course.

It would be worth taking on a load of mist coating just for the practice with the sprayer. This is a fairly acceptable thing to do and builders would expect you will be paid so much per house to mist coat it. If you like you can then carry on with the decorating in the normal fashion using a brush and roller.

You can spray woodwork too, you just need a smaller tip. This is a more advanced thing to do and unless you are very confident, I would get some experience spraying walls and ceilings first.

However, if you do decide to have a go at spraying woodwork then I suggest you prime bare wood first. This is pretty easy and again because it is new wood it is very absorbent and will tend not to run. If it does then it is only the prime coat so you can easily sand these runs out before you finish the woodwork off by brush.

The next step is actually spraying so let's hope you have a good surface to play on. Maybe a ceiling in your own house.

Above – A wall area sprayed with eggshell

Above – some oak doors ready to spray.

Step 6

Actually spraying

It's took us 5 steps to get to this point, but we are finally here! The best bit. This is where the fun starts.

Ideally you have plenty of area to play on. Maybe you have emptied a bedroom at home, and you are going to spray it out or maybe you are lucky enough to have got a full house of bare plaster that needs mist coating. Either way have plenty to go at so that you can practice properly.

The fear

Firstly, I know how you feel, I remember the first time I ever sprayed, and I was scared! I don't know why, the worse than can happen is that you get loads of runs and that's not the end of the world.

Once you have pulled that trigger and done a bit you will be fine, don't worry about it. In fact, make all your mistakes now and get them out of your system, experiment a little and see what happens.

It is very important that you get your technique right at the beginning, so that as you improve you are doing it right. There are a number of things to bear in mind.

Distance

The distance the gun is from the surface is very important. You should be between 8" and 12" from the surface. I spray a hand span away from the wall. I know this means depending on how big your hands are it could vary but a handspan is a great measure to remember.

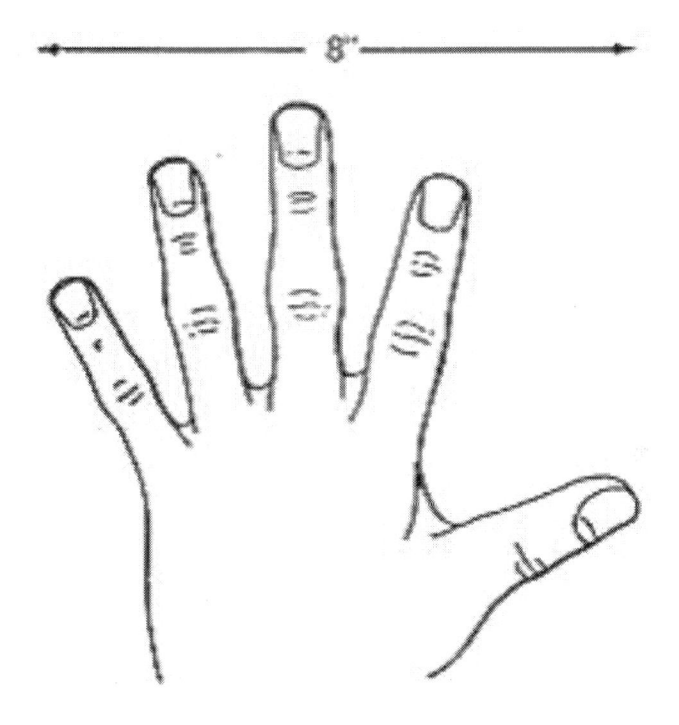

Above – A hand span

The beginner error here is to be too far away from the surface. I see so many people do this.

The problem is that although 18" from the surface does not seem much different to 12" it will make a big difference to your spraying.

Too far away causes loads of overspray especially with airless.

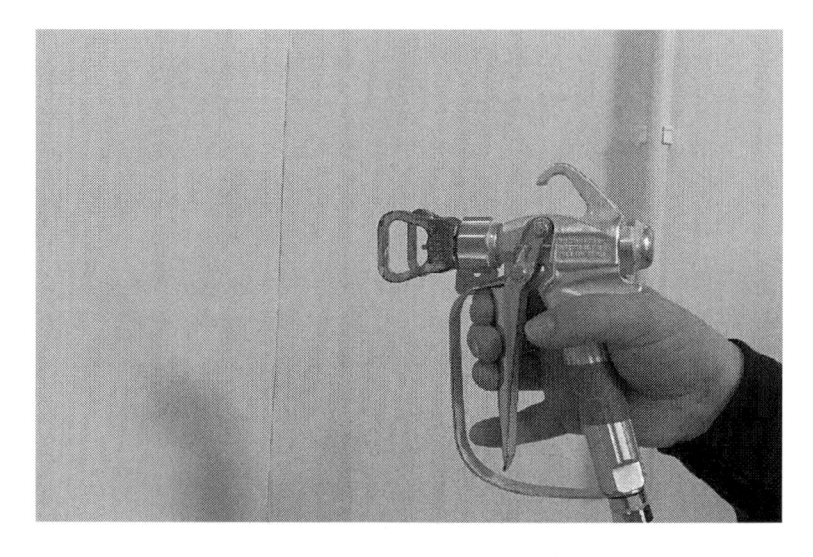

Above – The gun is a hand span from the surface

Fanning

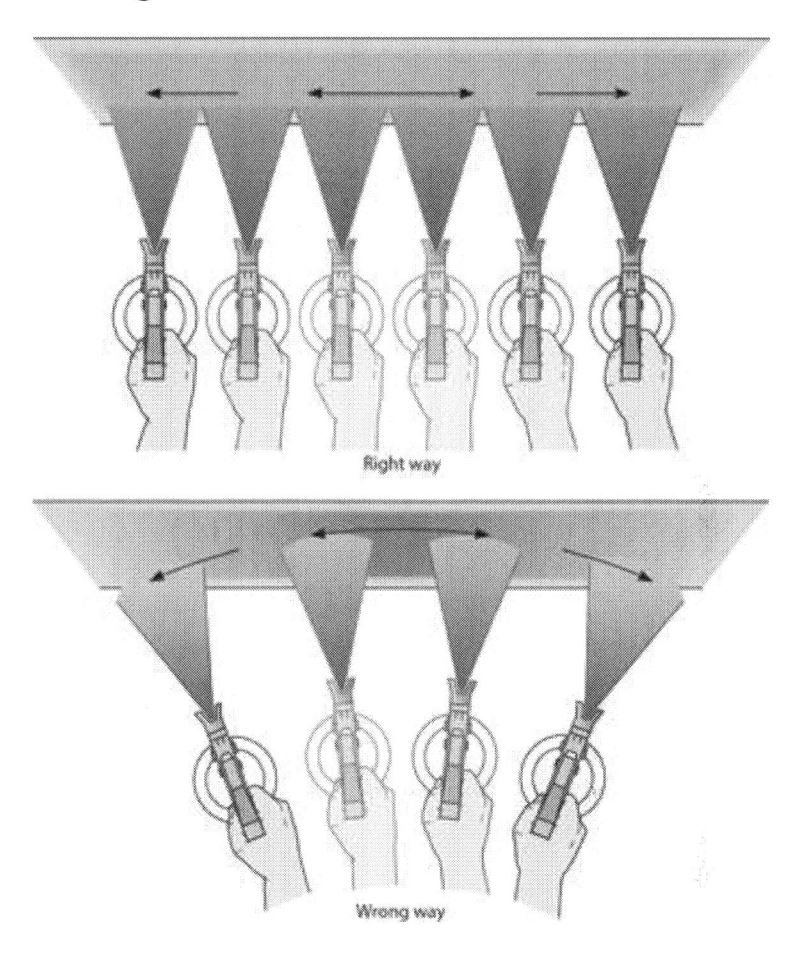

Right way

Wrong way

Fanning is where you do not keep parallel to the surface and you start waving your gun about. There are a couple of problems with this, you will get more overspray because you are spraying into the air at either side of the surface and also you will not get an even coating on the surface. The paint will be thicker in the middle and thinner at the edges.

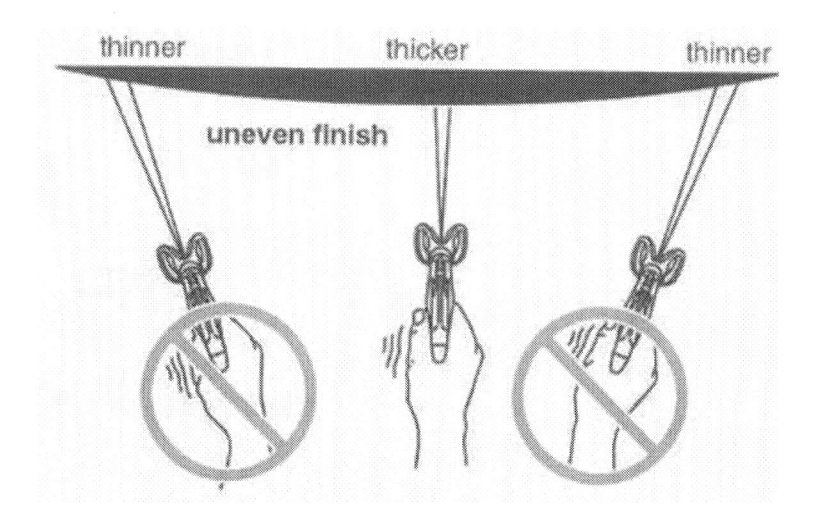

Above – Fanning gives you an uneven finish

It is so easy to spray like this because it "feels right" and your arm naturally arcs when you move it around.

Keeping the gun, the same distance from the surface feels very robotic. Once you get into it though it gets easier and easier.

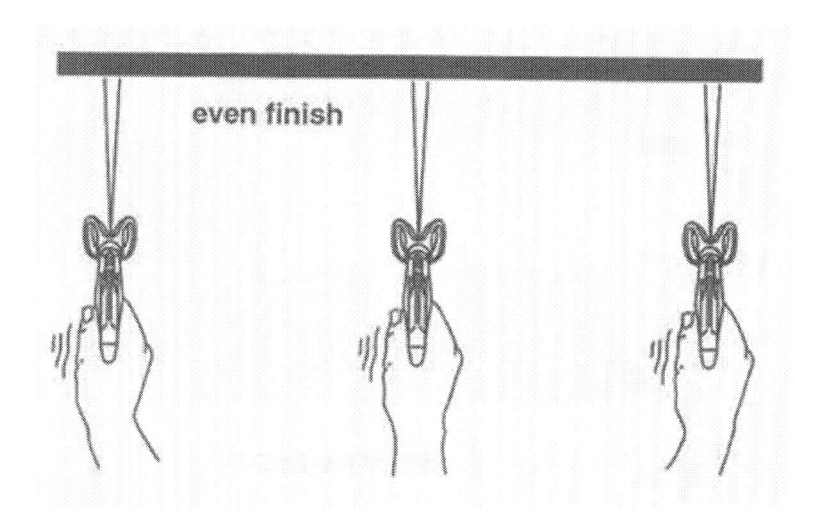

Above – perfect technique

Overlap

You need to overlap each stroke by 50%. This means that you spray a pass and then when you do the second pass you aim your gun at the edge of your first pass.

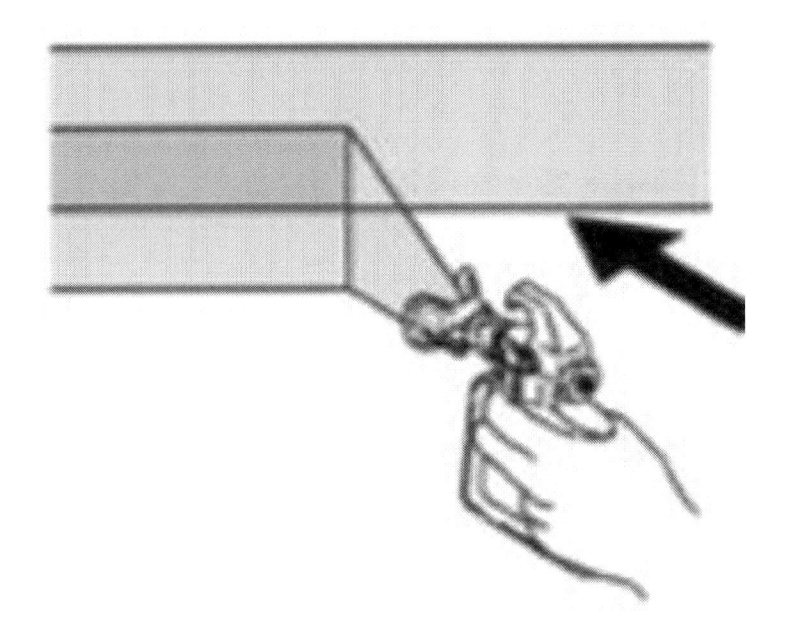

Above – overlap each stroke

Trigger on and trigger off

You need to trigger off at the end of each stroke. This does two things; it gives you a minute to look at what you have done and also it stops build up off paint at the end of each pass.

Some experienced sprayers will sometimes not trigger off (for various reasons) but if you are learning it is best not to try this. I would trigger on and trigger off until you get to the stage where you are really confident and then start trying the dodges.

Your speed

If you are not putting enough paint onto the wall when you spray then you are moving your gun too fast, you need to sow down a little.

If you are loading the paint on the wall and it is starting to run (more likely) then you need to speed up a little.

Experiment with your speed and see what difference it makes to the amount of paint that is put on the surface.

This will vary depending on the tip that you are using (more on this in a minute) but it's worth getting a real feel for how the speed that you move your gun affects the paint delivery.

Once you have chosen your tip then speed is the biggest way to control what you are doing. You will find that you settle into a "normal" speed for your style.

Tips and filters

I could write pages and pages about tips and filters, but I am not going to. At this stage you only need to know the basics.

If you have a brand-new sprayer and you are getting it out of the box, then it will come with everything that you need.

Usually, the sprayer will come with a 517 tip and a 50-mesh filter. The filter and the tip go together. I have found that people who have never sprayed before will struggle a little with a 517 tip, it is a bit fast. Before I go on let us quickly look at what the magic number means.

5 – This first part of the number is the **FAN WIDTH**. This is how wide the spray pattern is. You double the number, so that 5 would give you a 10-inch fan.

17 – This is the **SIZE OF THE HOLE**. It is measured in thousandths of an inch. 17 thou is a small hole. Put the tip up to the light and have a look at it. The bigger the hole the faster the paint comes out. The smaller the hole the slower it comes out.

If you want to go a bit slower for your first try, then get a smaller tip. If you buy Wagner tips, they come with the correct filter too. You could buy a 515 tip with a yellow (100 mesh) filter.

Above – pencil filters

If you have a Graco sprayer then you are better sticking with Graco tips, just remember to get a 100-mesh filter if you get a smaller tip.

Then have a day spraying, you will soon start to enjoy it. Experiment a little with speed and distance and get a feel for it. One last tip. It's worth videoing yourself and then watching it back.

What I found when teaching people how to spray is that they cannot see faults in their own technique while they are spraying but boy, they can spot the faults in everyone else.

Watch a video of yourself spraying and it's surprising what you will learn.

Step 7

Cleaning out the sprayer

This is the step that puts most decorators off spraying. They say, "is it worth getting the sprayer out for one ceiling because it takes a long time to clean it" or they say, "it took me nearly an hour to clean my sprayer the last time that I used it".

Before I carry on just let me say that I would rather clean out my sprayer than a roller any day. It's much easier and quicker, once you get used to it.

That's the thing, the first time that you clean out your sprayer it does seem like a big job, but the thousandth time will be a ten-minute doddle of a job.

There are a few things that decorators do wrong when cleaning out the sprayer and I will talk about them here but the main one is simply expecting the sprayer to stay looking brand new forever. I can understand this because I am a bit OCD when it comes to cleaning.

But I find now that when I clean the sprayer out on a job, I just do what is necessary and then once in a while (every year for me) I give the sprayer a really good spring clean to bring it back to its former glory.

Here are the steps to cleaning.

Step 1 – Organise a clean bucket, you will need these to make the process easier. Half fill the bucket with warm water.

Not too hot and not cold, just as warm as you would have your bath.

Step 2 – Put the return tube into the paint and pump the paint out of the hopper. It is worth having a brush handy at this point to clean off the sides of the hopper.

Step 3 – Pour warm water into the hopper.

Step 4 – Turn the pressure down so that the sprayer stops. Get the gun and point it onto the side of the bucket, pull the trigger. Then turn the prime/spray switch to spray and then turn the pressure up.

Notice that we pulled the trigger FIRST. This stops the pressure building up. Run the paint from the hose back into the paint tub. This usually takes about 30 seconds.

Once you start to get water coming out of the gun, transfer the gun to the bucket with wastewater in and let it run until all the water has gone from the hopper.

Turn the pressure down and switch back to prime, ready for the next step.

Step 5 – Now you need to clean out the filters. There are three. There is one at the bottom of the hopper and the easiest way to clean this is to screw it off and take it to the sink to clean.

Next is the manifold filter.

Not all sprayers have one but if yours does then screw it out and go and clean it in the sink. It should be pretty clean already. Once clean replace it onto the sprayer.

Finally take the pencil filter out of the gun and give it a good clean. Once clean replace it into the gun.

Just pause for a second at this point.

If you are going to be using the sprayer again the next day, then you can stop here.

The sprayer only has dirty water in it and all your filters are clean (this is important) so you can leave it overnight and put it back in paint the next day.

I call this a "dirty flush" and it takes around 5 minutes. If you are going to put the sprayer into storage for a while, then you will need to do a further clean flush.

This is the "clean flush"

Step 6 – Clean out the bucket that you have been using and half fill one with clean warm water.

Pour clean water into the hopper.

Step 7 – Switch to prime (if it's not already in prime), put the return tube into the empty clean bucket and turn the pressure up.

Run this until clean water comes out of the return tube. It won't take long, maybe a minute. Turn the pressure back down to zero.

Step 8 – Take the gun and pull the trigger. (FIRST like last time). Point the gun into the wastewater bucket and switch the spray. Turn the pressure up. Run this until clean water comes out of the gun.

This may take longer, maybe 2 or 3 minutes. Once clean, turn the pressure down and switch back to prime.

Just pause for a second again.

For most sprayers you will need to add pump guard at this point. This will stop the inside of the sprayer from rusting and also stop it freezing if the sprayer is kept in your van or the garage.

You are better having some pump guard mixed up in a ten-litre bucket with the lid on.

Step 9 – Pour the pump guard mix into the hopper and run the pump, this will circulate the fluid into the pump, and you will see blue fluid coming out of the return tube.

You should also circulate it through the hose too, but I never bother. See what is recommended for your sprayer.

As a final note on pump guard, my sprayer is a Tritech and has aerospace grade alloys in the pump that will not rust. I also keep the sprayer in a nice centrally heated house.

I never use pump guard. However, any other brand of sprayer will rust inside the pump if you do not use it. It's up to you.

Step 10 – Finally swich the sprayer off and put a couple of drops of throat seal liquid onto the piston to keep it lubricated.

Above – Throat seal liquid

Step 8

Thinking about accessories

We have come a long way. We have chosen a sprayer, bought one (I assume), set it up and sprayed with it. You feel a bit more confident spraying and now you are thinking about buying some extra "accessories" to make your spraying life a little easier.

When you buy a sprayer, everything that you need is in the box. You can unpack it, screw it all together and get spraying. However, you will soon find that there are a few accessories that are "essential" and some that are just handy to have.

Essential accessories

Whip hose

The high-pressure hose is pretty stiff and inflexible. When you are spraying you can find yourself fighting with it a little, especially if you are spraying intricate areas.

A whip hose is a short (usually a metre) length of flexible hose that goes between the main hose and the gun. You can actually get the whole hose in the same gauge as a whip hose and this would work fine in small workshop or domestic settings, but I don't think it would be tough enough for a site environment.

A whip hose is not expensive, and you can buy a standard one for between £20 and £30 depending on where you shop.

Above – A whip hose

Extension pole

When you first start spraying you will just use the gun without an extension on it. This helps you get used to the gun and how it handles. However, if you need to spray a higher ceiling then an extension pole is really handy. You will find that once you get used to using an extension pole you will find yourself using it more and more.

I use a short (12") extension pole when spraying walls, it makes the gun easier to use and you will not be doing as much bending and stretching. They are not expensive either and you can get cheap unbranded ones for around £20.

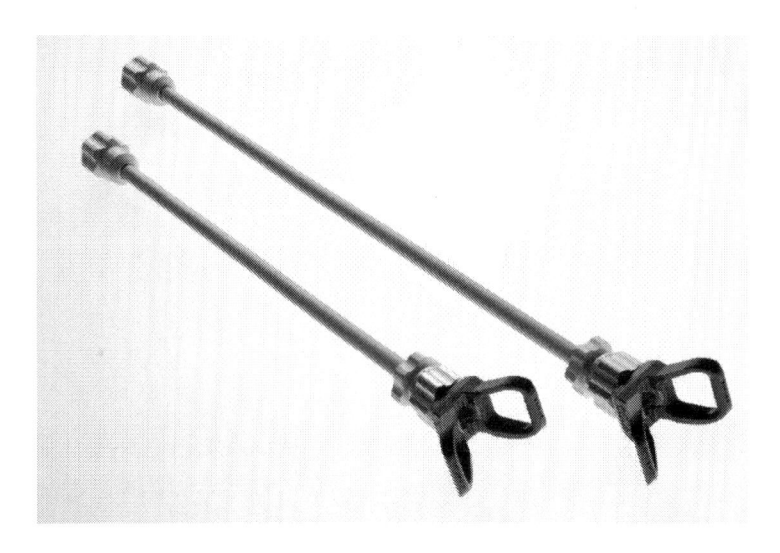

Above – Extension bars

Shorter hose

In most cases when you buy your sprayer it will come with a 15 metre (50 foot) hose. This is great when working in larger commercial properties but can get in the way a little on smaller jobs.

When working in someone's house I prefer a 7.5 metre hose. There are three advantages to this. The first one is that a shorter hose will hold less paint, around half a litre so this means you have less paint tied up while you are spraying. The second advantage is that the sprayer is quicker to clean out.

What most people don't realise with an airless sprayer is that the hose is the thing that takes the longest to clean out. The longer the hose the longer it will take to clean. The final advantage is that in a smaller area the hose can get in its own way a bit. It needs to be tamed. A smaller hose is easier to control than a longer one.

If you are working on a large site, you may find that you need a hose longer than 15 metres. You can easily connect two hoses together to make a

30-metre hose. All you need is a hose connector, and these are cheap, under a fiver.

Smaller tips

When you get your new sprayer, it will very likely come with a 517 tip. This is a great all rounder for spraying walls and ceilings. However, if you have never sprayed before it will be quite hard to handle as previously mentioned.

If you decide that you want to have a go at spraying woodwork, then you will need to buy a much smaller tip. The best time to buy these extra tips is when you buy your sprayer because the supplier will give you more discount. Many suppliers will do you a "bundle" of accessories for a great price.

I would get a 515 tip for starting off on walls and ceilings and a 310 tip for woodwork. Don't forget to get a pack of 100 mesh filters (they are only cheap) to use with these smaller tips.

Accessories nice to have

Cleanshot valve

When you add an extension pole to your gun there is a danger of spitting, this is where the gun carries on spraying for a second after you trigger off and you get a blob of paint on the surface.

It's not a massive problem but the longer the extension bar the worse the problem is.

The solution to this problem is the "Cleanshot" valve. This is a Graco accessory, but it will fit, and all makes of gun.

Above – the Cleanshot valve

Another advantage of the Cleanshot is that it is a swivel so that you can angle the tip any way you want. It can be very useful when spraying awkward areas.

The Cleanshot is around £150 but you get a Graco tip guard and tip with this as well and these are handy to have.

Hopper

Most sprayers come with a long suction tube connected to the pump on the sprayer. This is great for putting into large 20 litre buckets of paint. If you are spraying with smaller amounts though the suction tube can struggle.

It needs a couple of litres in the bucket to work and will suck air into the pump once the paint level gets low. It is also harder to move your sprayer around with the suction tube in a big bucket because you find yourself trying to carry both the bucket of paint and the sprayer.

The solution to this is a hopper.

You can buy these for any sprayer and you just take off the suction pipe and put on the hopper. They are interchangeable so you can swap back if you want. I usually set two sprayers up when I am doing a job.

One for the walls and ceiling and one for the woodwork. The woodwork sprayer will most likely use less than 5 litres of paint in the day. This sprayer is the one that I have a hopper fitted to.

It's great because it comes with a lid which keeps dust and debris out if the paint and also its easy to pick up the sprayer and move it about, even from job to job.

The price of a hopper will vary depending on the brand, but they are around £200.

Above – A Graco hopper

Above - A Tritech T5 with a hopper

You can see from the picture that the tube from the hopper screws onto the bottom of the sprayer. If you remove the hopper you can screw the suction tube (the large pipe on the picture on the following page) back on and then you can use the sprayer for spraying larger quantities of paint.

The return tube stays the same.

Above - A Tritech with the suction tube attached

Spray roller

The final accessory is a spray roller. These can be handy if you do a lot of large textured areas like blockwork. They can be a bit cumbersome and they are quite expensive, but they are out there and worth being aware of.

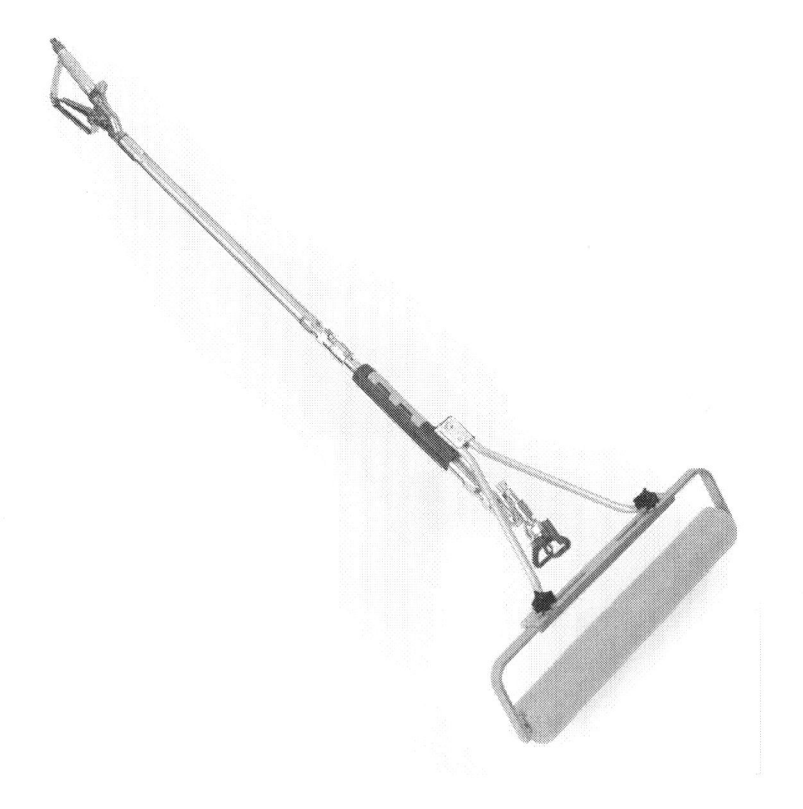

Above – The Graco jet roller

Finally

A short summary

It's great getting accessories for your sprayer especially if they make your life easier.

The main purpose for this guide is to keep it simple so I have not gone into too much detail. I just wanted to get you started.

If you want more information, I have included details of the books I have written on various topics for you to check out.

We run a private training academy that teaches decorators a range of skills including airless spraying. I have included some of our course leaflets at the back of this book.

Finally, it is worth knowing that you can claim CITB funding for courses. This is up to £5,000 for each year and the money can be used on any construction related courses for your business.

If you want information about courses or funding then email us at;-

courses@painttechtrainingacademy.co.uk

Glossary of terms

Airless sprayer

> This is a type of spray equipment that uses a high-pressure pump to spray paint. The paint is at 2000 psi when it comes out of the tip and this is enough to atomise it without the use of air.

Atomise

> This is when paint is broken into a fine mist and can therefore be sprayed.

Bounce back

> If you spray either too close to the surface or at too high a pressure then the paint can bounce back from the surface causing a type of overspray.

Cleanshot valve

> A device made by Graco which fits on the end of your extension pole to prevent spitting. This is an extra valve in the end of

the pole which shuts off the flow of paint when you release the trigger at the gun.

Diaphragm pump

A pump design, different from the piston pump (some would say better) which uses a flexible membrane and pulsating hydraulic fluid to produce pressure. Check out the Wagner Finish range.

Electronic pressure control

This regulates the pressure electronically rather than mechanically to provide a more precise control.

Fan size

The spray fan is the width of the spray pattern on the wall when the gun is 12" from the wall. This is shown by the first number on the tip. For example, 517 would give a 10" fan pattern. (Multiply the first number by two).

Fine finish tip

> This is a specially designed tip for better atomisation for use on surfaces where a better finish is needed such as doors and skirting. Wagner make a Fine Finish tip. Tritech make an Ultrafinish tip.

GPM

> Gallons per minute.

Inlet ball

> The ball part of the inlet valve of the fluid section of the airless sprayer. This acts as a check valve when sucking in paint. This can sometimes stick when the sprayer has been in storage.

Inlet tube

> This is the large tube that is put into the paint or material to be sprayed.

Orifice

> The hole in the tip that the paint passes through. This is a very small hole and is measured in thousandths of an inch. This is shown by the second part of the number stamped on the tip.
>
> For example 517 is a 17 thousandths of an inch orifice. The size of the hole controls the amount of paint that is put on the surface. The bigger the hole the more paint is put on.

Overspray

> This is where the paint in the form of a mist goes beyond the surface you are spraying and settles on something you don't want it too. Easily avoided by good technique and masking.

Packings

> The material used to make the piston liquid tight and therefore build pressure. These need changing every couple of years.

Pole

AKA extension pole, this screws on the end of your gun to give you more reach. Available in several sizes. These can be used to paint ceilings or to make spraying walls easier. These can be screwed together to give extra reach if needed.

Pressure roller

This is a roller that fits on the end of an extension pole and is fed paint by the airless sprayer. This eliminates the need to keep dipping the roller in paint and in theory creates less overspray.

Priming

This is where you charge the pump with paint and remove air from the system so that the pressure can be built up. Usually done when setting up but may need to be done if you run out of paint while spraying and draw in air.

Pump armour

> A liquid that is put into the pump that protects it from frost and rust while in storage. Similar to antifreeze in a car engine.

Return tube

> The smaller tube that returns the material back into the paint container when the pump is in prime mode.

Spray fan

> The pattern that the sprayer makes when spraying. Usually a sharp line. This will soften to an oval when worn.

Spray tip

> This slots into the tip guard and is the business end of the airless sprayer. This controls the fan width and the amount of paint sprayed onto the surface. These wear and need to be changed when worn.

Throat seal liquid

> AKA "TSL" This is a lubricant that is placed in a small cup at the top of the piston to keep the packings wet and lubricated. This needs to be done every four hours of continuous use.

Viscosity

> This is how thick or thin the paint is and is measured with a viscosity cup which allows you to time the speed that paint flows. The faster it flows the thinner it is.

Whip hose.

> A thinner flexible piece of hose between the end of the high-pressure hose and the gun. This is more flexible and makes for an easier day spraying.

All prices are correct at the time of printing (April 2021) and are reviewed every April.

PAINTTECH TRAINING ACADEMY

INTENSIVE AIRLESS SPRAYING

PRICE: £560 +VAT
(PER PERSON, MAXIMUM 6 IN A GROUP)

DURATION: 2 DAYS

LOCATION: EDENBRIDGE, CREDITON, PRESTON, GLENROTHES & CASTLEBAR

COURSE CONTENT:
The course is mainly practical, on the first day you will spend the morning in the classroom going through all the Health & Safety and theory aspects before moving into the workshop. Practical assessment takes place throughout the duration of the course and there is a short theory test at the end of day 2.

On successful completion of the course you will be awarded with a City & Guilds certificate, and you will also receive a digital credential which you can use on your website and across social media platforms.

You will cover all the main concepts such as:
- Basic Health & Safety
- Masking & De-masking
- Mindset & Objections
- Equipment set up & clean down
- Spray technique
- Different tips & accessories
- Common mistakes
- Products
- Tip sizes for use with trim
- Pressure/product/tip size combinations Systems

WEB: www.painttechtrainingacademy.co.uk
EMAIL: courses@painttechtrainingacademy.co.uk

This is ideal for a beginner who wants to get into airless spraying.

All prices are correct at the time of printing (April 2021) and are reviewed every April.

PAINTTECH TRAINING ACADEMY

INTRODUCTION TO HVLP

PRICE: £285 +VAT
(PER PERSON, MAXIMUM 6 IN A GROUP)

DURATION: 1 DAY

LOCATION: EDENBRIDGE, CREDITON, PRESTON, GLENROTHES & CASTLEBAR

You will cover all the main concepts such as:
- Use of HVLP gravity fed & suction cup guns plus needle setting
- Use of pressure pots
- Conventional spraying using compressor
- Products
- Pressures and products with the different machines
- Spraying techniques
- Cleaning maintenance
- Fault finding

COURSE CONTENT:

The course is a 100% practical day.

This course is designed to show you how to get the best possible finish with your HVLP/LVLP or compressor set up. We look at all the different options, including pressure pots, compressors, HVLP machines, different needle sets and different types of guns.

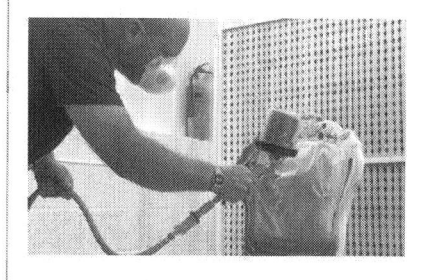

WEB - www.painttechtrainingacademy.co.uk   EMAIL - courses@painttechtrainingacademy.co.uk

This course is ideal for a decorator who wants to spray small items or get into uPVC spraying.

All prices are correct at the time of printing (April 2021) and are reviewed every April.

PAINTING USING HVLP EQUIPMENT

PRICE: £535 +VAT
(PER PERSON, MAXIMUM 6 IN A GROUP)

DURATION: 2 DAYS

LOCATION: EDENBRIDGE, CREDITON, PRESTON, GLENROTHES & CASTLEBAR

You will cover all the main concepts such as:
- Health & Safety
- Use of HVLP gravity fed & suction cup guns plus needle setting
- Use of pressure pots
- Conventional spraying using compressor
- Checking the suitability of previously prepared surfaces
- Pressures and products with the different machines
- Spraying techniques
- Cleaning & maintenance
- Fault finding

COURSE CONTENT:

The course is 20% classroom/theory and 80% practical training.

This course is designed to show you how to get the best possible finish with your HVLP/LVLP or compressor set up. We look at all the different options, including pressure pots, compressors, HVLP machines, different needle sets and different types of guns. With 80% of this course over 2 days being practical you get a lot of time practicing your spray technique and learning how to correctly use the equipment.

WEB - www.painttechtrainingacademy.co.uk
EMAIL - courses@painttechtrainingacademy.co.uk

This is a more in depth 2-day course looking at both HVLP and conventional spraying systems.

All prices are correct at the time of printing (April 2021) and are reviewed every April.

PAINTTECH TRAINING ACADEMY

KITCHEN & FURNITURE ONSITE SPRAYING

PRICE: £280 +VAT
(PER PERSON, MAXIMUM 5 IN A GROUP)

DURATION: 1 DAY

LOCATION: EDENBRIDGE, CREDITON, PRESTON, GLENROTHES & CASTLEBAR

You will cover all the main concepts such as:

- Products – water based, solvent based, acid cat, PU's and cellulose products
- Combination of workshop & on site set ups
- Pressures and products with the different machines
- Tips, tricks & masking techniques
- Spraying techniques
- Cleaning & maintenance
- Fault finding

Approved Training Organisation — citb — PAINTTECH

COURSE CONTENT:

The course is a 100% practical day.

You will spray fitted furniture similar to that you would find on site, for example kitchen units & fitted shelving. You will be taught how to get an amazing finish on fitted furniture using various spray methods. This course is using the airless system it does not cover HVLP or compressor & you have to have completed the intro to spraying as a prerequisite to this course.

WEB - www.painttechtrainingacademy.co.uk
EMAIL - courses@painttechtrainingacademy.co.uk

This is designed for decorators that want to get into kitchen spraying.

All prices are correct at the time of printing (April 2021) and are reviewed every April.

PAINTTECH TRAINING ACADEMY

AIRLESS SPRAY PLASTER APPLICATION AND FINISHING

PRICE: £605 +VAT
(PER PERSON, MAXIMUM 5 IN A GROUP)

DURATION: 2 DAYS

LOCATION: EDENBRIDGE, CREDITON, PRESTON, GLENROTHES

On successful completion of the course you will be awarded with a City & Guilds certificate, and you will also receive a digital credential which you can use on your website and across social media platforms.

COURSE CONTENT:

The course is mainly a practical day. Approximately 10% of the day is spent in the classroom and 90% is spent in the workshop.

After being taught how to tape & joint, you will then spray walls and ceilings with the airless plaster, and then be shown how to turn this into an amazing level 5 finish.

You will cover all the main concepts such as:
- Products & suppliers
- Machines & tools
- Taping & Jointing
- External corners
- Internal corners
- Walls
- Ceilings
- Spatulas trowels

WEB - www.painttechtrainingacademy.co.uk   EMAIL - courses@painttechtrainingacademy.co.uk

This course explores airless spray plaster. This is the future of plastering and will be the topic of one of my "simple steps" books.

All prices are correct at the time of printing (April 2021) and are reviewed every April.

PAINTTECH TRAINING ACADEMY
PAPER HANGING INTRODUCTION

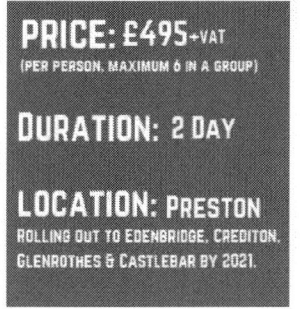

PRICE: £495 +VAT
(PER PERSON, MAXIMUM 6 IN A GROUP)

DURATION: 2 DAY

LOCATION: PRESTON
ROLLING OUT TO EDENBRIDGE, CREDITON, GLENROTHES & CASTLEBAR BY 2021.

COURSE CONTENT:
This is a two-day course aimed at people who have little or no experience of wallpapering. You will learn the basics including preparing the wall to receive wallpaper, the tools that would use and what to look for when buying wallpapering tools. You will also hang foundation papers to ceilings and walls. On the second day you will hang non-matching vinyl wallpaper to walls in a variety of situations. The emphasis will be on developing good skills that you can build on in the workplace.

- Adopt safe and healthy work practices, procedures and skills relating to the method/area of work.
- Use methods of calculating quantity, length, area and wastage associate with the method/procedure to hang wallcoverings.
- Check suitability of surfaces to receive wallpaper. This will involve looking at different surfaces and discussing how you would treat them before hanging wallpaper.
- Preparation of pastes and adhesives. You will look at a range of pastes and discuss what they are used for, this will include cellulose paste, starch pastes and ready mixed paste.
- Prepare and hang foundation paper, textured/relief finishing papers wallcoverings to walls.
- Work around electrical fittings and pipework.
- Safe use of access equipment, hand tools and associated equipment.

Approved Training Organisation **citb** **PAINT TECH** TRAINING ACADEMY

WEB - www.painttechtrainingacademy.co.uk   EMAIL - courses@painttechtrainingacademy.co.uk

All prices are correct at the time of printing (April 2021) and are reviewed every April.

PAINTTECH TRAINING ACADEMY

PAPER HANGING INTERMEDIATE

PRICE: £495 +VAT
(PER PERSON, MAXIMUM 4 IN A GROUP)

DURATION: 2 DAYS

LOCATION: PRESTON
ROLLING OUT TO EDENBRIDGE, CREDITON, GLENROTHES & CASTLEBAR BY 2021.

COURSE CONTENT:

This course is designed for people who have either done the paperhanging introduction and want to further improve their skills or someone who has done some wallpapering in industry and want to further their skills. The course will cover pattern papers and various types of wallpaper including non-woven, vinyl and traditional wallpapers. You will hang wallpaper in a range of settings including walls, ceilings, window reveals and a fireplace surround. You will be taught how to measure up these areas for wallpaper and how to handle different types of Pattern match.

- Adopt safe and healthy work practices, procedures and skills relating to the method/area of work
- Use methods of calculating quantity, length, area, and wastage associate with the method/procedure to hang wallcoverings
- Check suitability of surfaces to receive wallpaper.
- Preparation of pastes and adhesives.
- Prepare and hang the following: -Patterned vinyl, Non-woven, Traditional paper
- To the following surfaces: – Walls, Ceilings, Window reveal, Fireplace
- Work around electrical fittings
- Safe use of access equipment, hand tools and associated equipment

Approved Training Organisation — citb — PAINTTECH TRAINING ACADEMY

WEB - www.painttechtrainingacademy.co.uk   EMAIL - courses@painttechtrainingacademy.co.uk

All prices are correct at the time of printing (April 2021) and are reviewed every April.

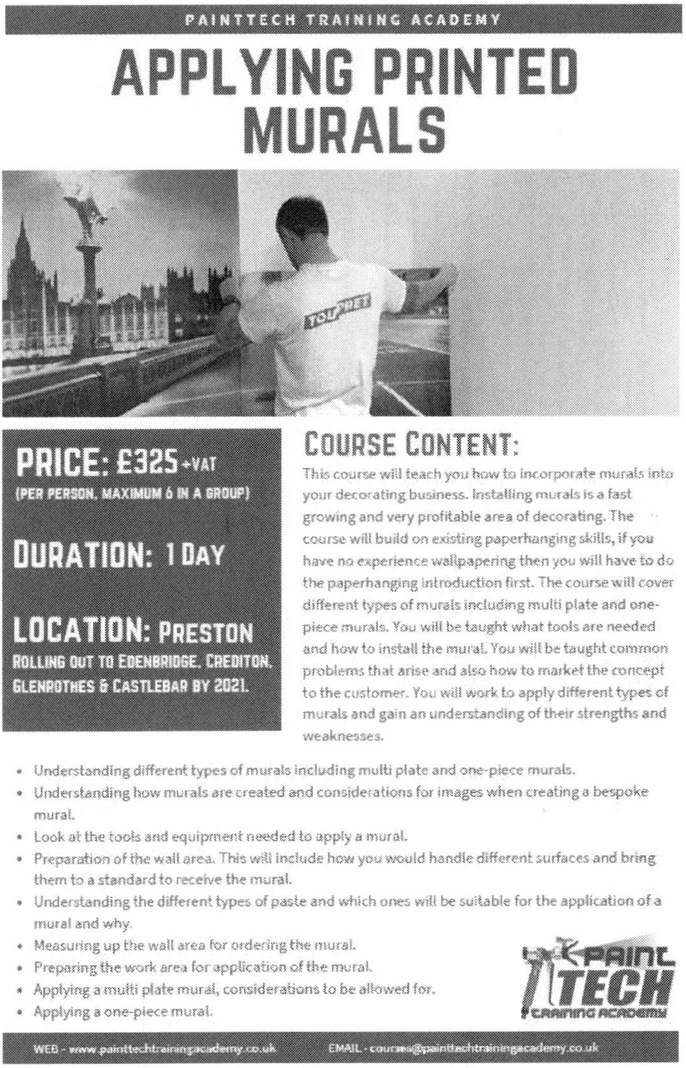

PAINTTECH TRAINING ACADEMY
APPLYING PRINTED MURALS

PRICE: £325 +VAT
(PER PERSON, MAXIMUM 6 IN A GROUP)

DURATION: 1 DAY

LOCATION: PRESTON
ROLLING OUT TO EDENBRIDGE, CREDITON, GLENROTHES & CASTLEBAR BY 2021.

COURSE CONTENT:
This course will teach you how to incorporate murals into your decorating business. Installing murals is a fast growing and very profitable area of decorating. The course will build on existing paperhanging skills, if you have no experience wallpapering then you will have to do the paperhanging introduction first. The course will cover different types of murals including multi plate and one-piece murals. You will be taught what tools are needed and how to install the mural. You will be taught common problems that arise and also how to market the concept to the customer. You will work to apply different types of murals and gain an understanding of their strengths and weaknesses.

- Understanding different types of murals including multi plate and one-piece murals.
- Understanding how murals are created and considerations for images when creating a bespoke mural.
- Look at the tools and equipment needed to apply a mural.
- Preparation of the wall area. This will include how you would handle different surfaces and bring them to a standard to receive the mural.
- Understanding the different types of paste and which ones will be suitable for the application of a mural and why.
- Measuring up the wall area for ordering the mural.
- Preparing the work area for application of the mural.
- Applying a multi plate mural, considerations to be allowed for.
- Applying a one-piece mural.

PAINTTECH TRAINING ACADEMY

WEB - www.painttechtrainingacademy.co.uk   EMAIL - courses@painttechtrainingacademy.co.uk

There is a big market for specialist murals ad this course is designed for decorators who have no experience of installing murals

Other books by the author

The **"Fast and Flawless" series of books** is made up of three books. They can be read in any order, but I recommend that you read them as follows.

Fast and flawless – A guide to airless spraying. First learn about spraying.

Fast and flawless pricing – Once that you get more productive by spraying then you need to learn about how to start pricing correctly.

Fast and Flawless systems – Finally, and this is the real "secret" you need to put systems in place so that you become even more productive.

Fast and Flawless
A guide to airless spraying

This is a chatty guide to airless spraying for decorators, decorating students and anyone interested in spraying with an airless system.

The book covers all aspects of the airless sprayer including the components of the system, the different sprayers that are out there to buy and setting up the sprayer.

The book also covers topics such as types of sprayers, essential equipment, using the equipment, masking, PPE and masks, a bit about paint and finally what to do when it all goes wrong, spraying in the real world and common paint defects.

Fast and Flawless Pricing
A guide to pricing and business for decorators

Are you a decorator that struggles with pricing?

Have you just set up in business and are looking for some pointers?

Are you an established business looking for some inspiration on how to move forward?

This chatty guide on pricing and business will gently guide you through the process of pricing a decorating job. It looks at the pitfalls of getting your pricing wrong and the advantages of having a good pricing system.

The book has been written by someone who has both been a decorator and taught decorating in a local college for most of his life.

Fast and Flawless Systems
A Decorators guide to planning and carrying out successful job

This book looks at systems for Decorators.

This book covers all types of systems from which paint to use on what surface to what order you should spray a room. The book also covers aspects of decorating that you may or may not be aware of such as painting uPvc, training, funding and marketing.

If you have read the other two books already then this is one is a must read, if you haven't then this book is a great place to start.

Check out the website

If you are interested in being kept up to date with future books, or you just fancy the odd freebie, then subscribe on my website.

www.fastandflawless.co.uk

About the author

Pete Wilkinson has been a decorator all of his life. In his younger years he worked for a medium sized decorating company doing a wide range of work.

Then at the age of 27 he got a job teaching Painting and Decorating at a local college. These days he runs his own training company called PaintTech Training Academy.

When he is not working, he likes to spend time relaxing on his boat with his wife Tracey.

Printed in Great Britain
by Amazon